You are a constant reminder
of the beauty in my life

A quilt is
a lovely thing.

Daisies

A Quilted Gift For You

Sending You a
Rainbow

Test Pattern

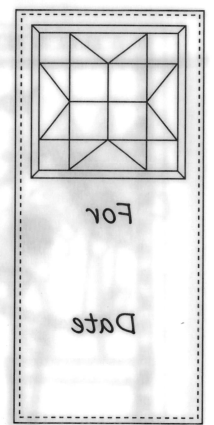

For You

A quilt for you because you are special to me.

Your friendship is a gift.

A Quilted Gift For You

Date

Test Pattern

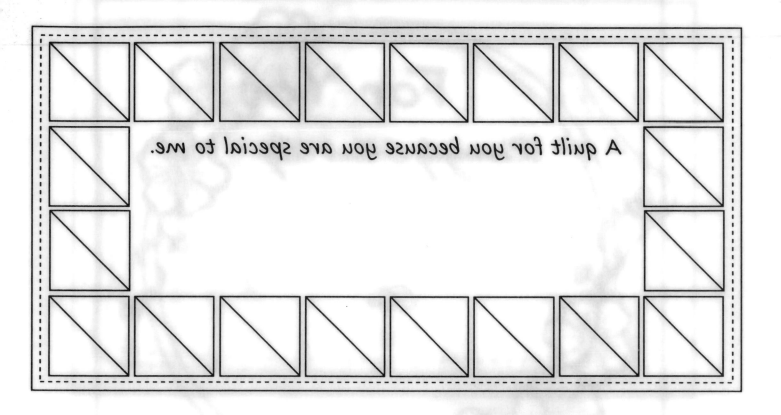

A quilt for you because you are special to me.

Your friendship is a gift.

A quilt for you because you are special to me.

Your friendship is a gift.

May this simple gift bring a smile to your face.

Lovingly Made By

For

May this simple gift bring
a smile to your face.

Test Pattern

Beautifully Behind & Light
lovelle wishes

For

Date

Wishing brings Y May this smile are bring
a smile to your face.

Star Pattern

Sending you
love & wishes

Date

Whooo Loves You?

I do!

Test Pattern

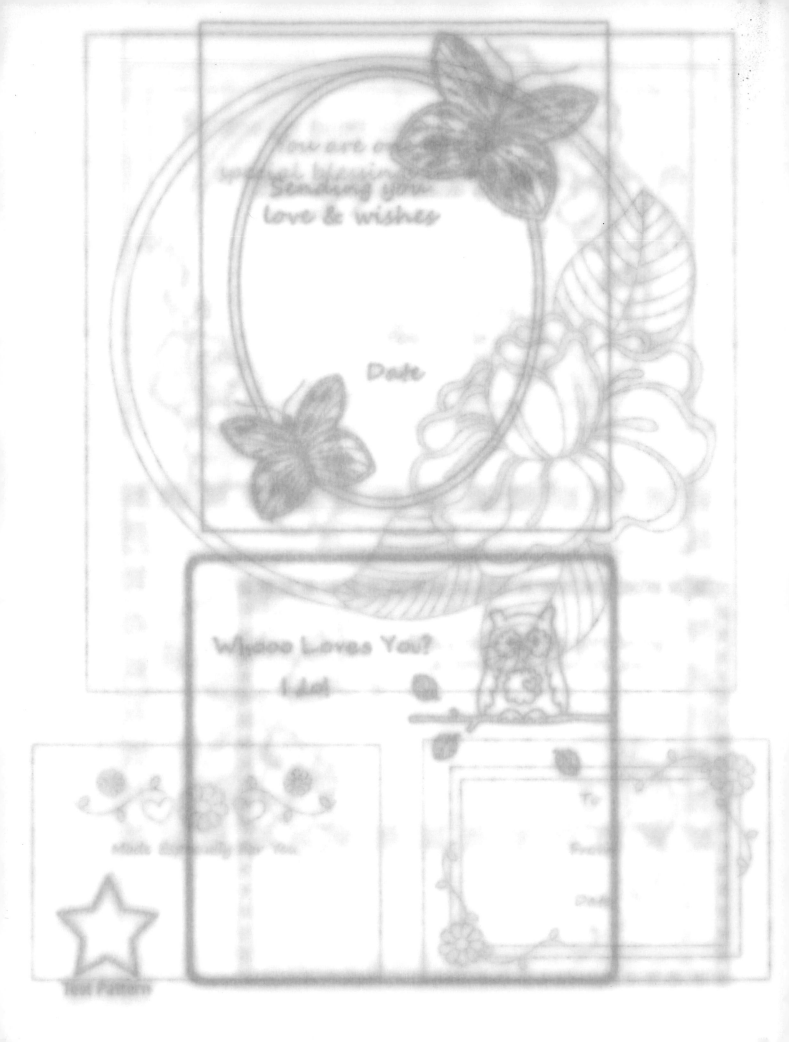

You are one of the
special blessings in my life.

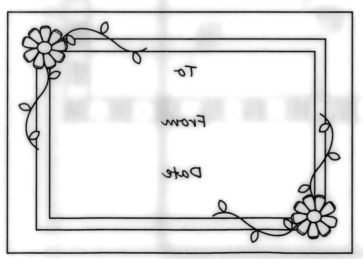

To

From

Date

Made Especially For You

Kittens are sweet, and so are you!

Puggies are special,
just like you!

Kittens are sweet, and so are you!

May the Joys of Christmas Fill Your Home and Your House.

Puppies are special,
just like you!

Made with Love By

May the Joys of Christmas Fill Your Heart & Your Home.

Made with Love By

For

May the Joy of Christmas Fill Your Heart & Your Home.

Made with Love By

A gift makes
everyone feel better!
For

Made Just For You

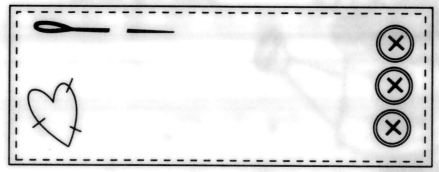

A quilt makes
everyone feel better!

Test Pattern

May love fill your home
today and always

Made Just For You

You bring
sunshine & showers
into my life

A gift makes
everyone feel better!

Made For

By

May love fill your home today and always.

You bring sunshine & flowers into my life.

Made For

By

Test Pattern

May love fill your home
today and always. Little Christmas

A quilt just for You bring
sunshine & flowers
into my live.

Made For

Date

By

Have Yourself
a Merry Little Christmas.

A quilt just for you

From

Date

Test Pattern

a Merry Little Christmas.
A baby has a special way
of adding joy...

A quilt just for you

From

Date

A baby has a special way
of adding joy.

Babies are blessings from Heaven above.

A baby has a special way
of adding joy.

Babies are blessings from Heaven above.

You Are A Blessing To Me!

You Are My Sunshine!

Thinking of You

Made With Love For You

In Honor of Your New Baby

Thinking of You

... are the patchwork of life.

Made With Love For You

Celebrating You

In Honor of Your New Baby

Test Pattern

Friends are the patchwork of life.

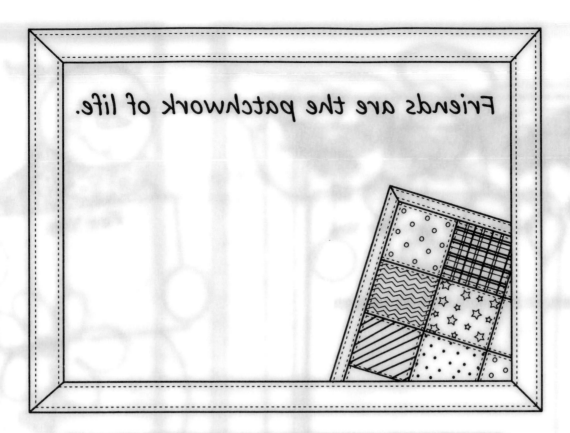

Celebrating You

Test Pattern

Friends are the patchwork of life.

believe in your wildest dreams

For You

Celebrating You

There is always something to be thankful for
and I'm thankful for you.

For You

believe in the magic of the season

There is always something to be thankful for ...
and I'm thankful for you.

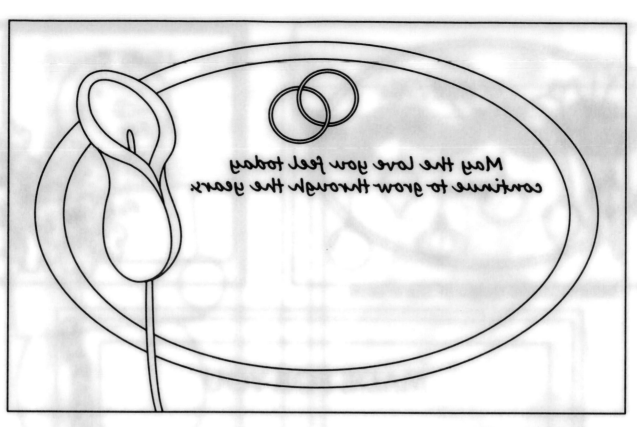

May the love you feel today
continue to grow through the years

Sisters are the blooms in the
garden of life.

May the love you find today
continue to grow through the years.

MADE FOR YOU

Sisters are the blooms in the
garden of life.

For

From

Made By

For

A Gift For

Date

MADE FOR YOU

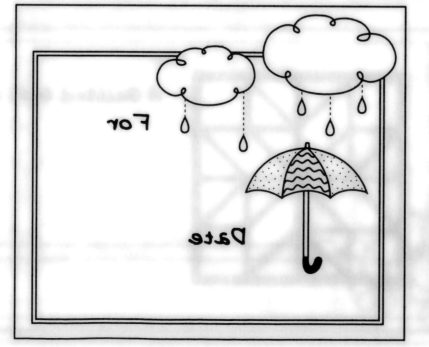

For

Date

Test Pattern

May today be filled
with sunshine & quilts!

MADE FOR YOU

A Quilted Gift for You

For

May today be filled
with sunshine & quilts!

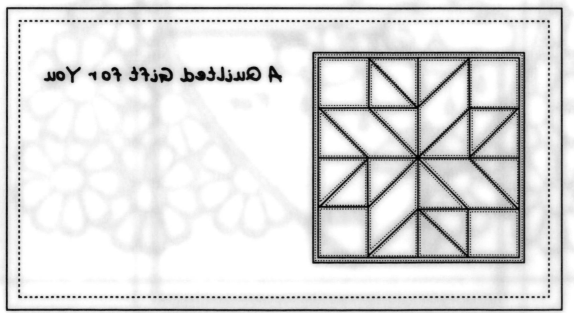

A Quilted Gift for You

Test Pattern

May today be filled
with sunshine & quilts!

...your lives & love
...ily ever after

A Quilter's Birthday Wish

May you live & love
happily ever after.

A Gift of Love

Thank you for your support!

May you live & love
happily ever after.

God Bless America

A Gift of Love

Thank You For Your Service!

God Bless America!

Test Pattern

Thank You For Your Service!

God Bless America!

A Joyful Gift Just for You

Hugs & Prayers
From Someone Who Cares

A Joyful Gift Just for You

Test Pattern

A quilt Hugs & Prayers
from Someone Who Cares

May angels watch over
& protect you always.

A Joyful Gift Just for You

A quilt for you because
you are special

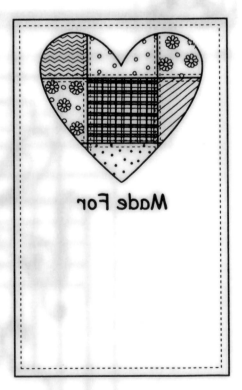

Made For

May angels watch over
& protect you always.

Test Pattern

A quilt for you because
you are special

Lovingly

For

May angels watch over
& protect you always.

Made For